VALUE PRICE AND PROFIT

KARL MARX

GENERAL PRESS

Published by
GENERAL PRESS
4805/24, Fourth Floor, Krishna House
Ansari Road, Daryaganj, New Delhi - 110002
Ph : 011-23282971, 45795759
E-mail : generalpressindia@gmail.com

www.generalpress.in

First Edition : 2022

ISBN : 9789354993978

Published by Azeem Ahmad Khan for General Press

Contents

BESTSELLING NON-FICTION

- Annihilation of Caste by Dr B.R. Ambedkar
  Social Science, ISBN: 9789390492732
- Believe in Yourself by Joseph Murphy
  Self-Help/Motivational, ISBN: 9789388118385
- How I Made $2,000,000 in the Stock Market by Nicolas Darvas
  Self-Help, ISBN: 9789389716283
- How to Attract Money by Joseph Murphy
  Self-Help, ISBN: 9789388118408
- How to Enjoy Your Life and Your Job by Dale Carnegie
  Self-Help, ISBN: 9789387669017
- How to Stop Worrying and Start Living by Dale Carnegie
  Self-Help, ISBN: 9789380914817
- How to Win Friends and Influence People by Dale Carnegie
  Self-Help, ISBN: 9788180320217
- Jail Diary and Other Writings by Bhagat Singh
  Biographies & Memoirs, ISBN: 9789390492398
- Know Your Worth by NK Sondhi & Vibha Malhotra
  Self-Help/Motivational, ISBN: 9788180320231
- Meditations by Marcus Aurelius
  Philosophy, ISBN: 9789388118736
- My Experiments with Truth by Mahatma Gandhi
  Biographies & Memoirs, ISBN: 9789387669291
- My Inventions: The Autobiography of Nikola Tesla
  Biographies & Memoirs, ISBN: 9789388118132

Search the book by its ISBN

Preface

The circumstances under which this paper was read are narrated at the beginning of the work. The paper was never published during the lifetime of Marx. It was found amongst his papers after the death of Engels. Among many other characteristics of Marx, this paper shows two especially. These are his patient willingness to make the meaning of his ideas plain to the humblest student, and the extraordinary clearness of those ideas. In a partial sense the present volume is an epitome of the first volume of Capital. More than one of us have attempted to analyse and simplify that volume, with not too much success perhaps. In fact, a witty friend and commentator has suggested that what is now required is an explanation by Marx of our explanations of him. I am often asked what is the best succession of books for the student to acquire the fundamental principles of Socialism. The question is a difficult one to answer. But, by way of suggestion, one might say, first, Engels' *Socialism, Scientific And Utopian*, then the present work, the first volume of Capital, and the Student's Marx. My small part in the preparation of this work has been reading the manuscript, making a few suggestions as to English forms of expression, dividing the work up into chapters and naming the chapters, and revising the proofs for press. All the rest, and by far the most important part, of the work has been done by her whose name appears on the title page. The present volume has already been translated into German.

–Edward Aveling

Preliminary

CITIZENS,

Before entering into the subject-matter, allow me to make a few preliminary remarks. There reigns now on the Continent a real epidemic of strikes, and a general clamour for a rise of wages. The question will turn up at our Congress. You, as the head of the International Association, ought to have settled convictions upon this paramount question. For my own part, I considered it therefore my duty to enter fully into the matter, even at the peril of putting your patience to a severe test.

Another preliminary remark I have to make in regard to Citizen Weston. He has not only proposed to you, but has publicly defended, in the interest of the working class, as he thinks, opinions he knows to be most unpopular with the working class. Such an exhibition of moral courage all of us must highly honour. I hope that, despite the unvarnished style of my paper, at its conclusion he will find me agreeing with what appears to me the just idea lying at the bottom of his theses, which, however, in their present form, I cannot but consider theoretically false and practically dangerous.

I shall now at once proceed to the business before us.

in population it must be so, because of the continuous change in the accumulation of capital and the productive powers of labour. It is perfectly true that if a rise in the general rate of wages should take place today, that rise, whatever its ulterior effects might be, would, by itself, not immediately change the amount of production. It would, in the first instance, proceed from the existing state of things. But if before the rise of wages the national production was variable, and not fixed, it will continue to be variable and not fixed after the rise of wages.

But suppose the amount of national production to be constant instead of variable. Even then, what our friend Weston considers a logical conclusion would still remain a gratuitous assertion. If I have a given number, say eight, the absolute limits of this number do not prevent its parts from changing their relative limits. If profits were six and wages two, wages might increase to six and profits decrease to two, and still the total amount remain eight. The fixed amount of production would by no means prove the fixed amount of wages. How then does our friend Weston prove this fixity? By asserting it.

But even conceding him his assertion, it would cut both ways, while he presses it only in one direction. If the amount of wages is a constant magnitude, then it can be neither increased nor diminished. If then, in enforcing a temporary rise of wages, the working men act foolishly, the capitalists, in enforcing a temporary fall of wages, would act not less foolishly. Our friend Weston does not deny that, under certain circumstances, the working men *can* enforce a rise of wages, but their amount being naturally fixed, there must follow a reaction. On the other hand, he knows also that the capitalists

Preliminary

CITIZENS,

Before entering into the subject-matter, allow me to make a few preliminary remarks. There reigns now on the Continent a real epidemic of strikes, and a general clamour for a rise of wages. The question will turn up at our Congress. You, as the head of the International Association, ought to have settled convictions upon this paramount question. For my own part, I considered it therefore my duty to enter fully into the matter, even at the peril of putting your patience to a severe test.

Another preliminary remark I have to make in regard to Citizen Weston. He has not only proposed to you, but has publicly defended, in the interest of the working class, as he thinks, opinions he knows to be most unpopular with the working class. Such an exhibition of moral courage all of us must highly honour. I hope that, despite the unvarnished style of my paper, at its conclusion he will find me agreeing with what appears to me the just idea lying at the bottom of his theses, which, however, in their present form, I cannot but consider theoretically false and practically dangerous.

I shall now at once proceed to the business before us.

1

Production and Wages

Citizen Weston's argument rested, in fact, upon two premises: firstly, the amount of national production is a fixed thing, a constant quantity or magnitude, as the mathematicians would say; secondly, that the amount of real wages, that is to say, of wages as measured by the quantity of the commodities they can buy, is a fixed amount, a constant magnitude.

Now, his first assertion is evidently erroneous. Year after year you will find that the value and mass of production increase, that the productive powers of the national labour increase, and that the amount of money necessary to circulate this increasing production continuously changes. What is true at the end of the year, and for different years compared with each other, is true for every average day of the year. The amount or magnitude of national production changes continuously. It is not a constant but a variable magnitude, and apart from changes in population it must be so, because of the continuous change in the accumulation of capital and the productive powers of labour. It is perfectly true that if a rise in the general rate of wages should take place today, that rise, whatever its ulterior effects might be, would, by itself, not immediately change the amount of production. It would, in the first instance, proceed from the existing state of things. But if before the rise of wages the national production was variable, and not fixed, it will continue to be variable and not fixed after the rise of wages.

But suppose the amount of national production to be constant instead of variable. Even then, what our friend Weston considers a logical conclusion would still remain a gratuitous assertion. If I have a given number, say eight, the absolute limits of this number do not prevent its parts from changing their relative limits. If profits were six and wages two, wages might increase to six and profits decrease to two, and still the total amount remain eight. The fixed amount of production would by no means prove the fixed amount of wages. How then does our friend Weston prove this fixity? By asserting it.

But even conceding him his assertion, it would cut both ways, while he presses it only in one direction. If the amount of wages is a constant magnitude, then it can be neither increased nor diminished. If then, in enforcing a temporary rise of wages, the working men act foolishly, the capitalists, in enforcing a temporary fall of wages, would act not less foolishly. Our friend Weston does not deny that, under certain circumstances, the working men *can* enforce a rise of wages, but their amount being naturally fixed, there must follow a reaction. On the other hand, he knows also that the capitalists *can* enforce a fall of wages, and, indeed, continuously try to enforce it. According to the principle of the constancy of wages, a reaction ought to follow in this case not less than in the former. The working men, therefore, reacting against the attempt at, or the act of, lowering wages, would act rightly. They would, therefore, act rightly in enforcing *a rise of wages*, because every *reaction* against the lowering of wages is an *action* for raising wages. According to Citizen Weston's own principle of the *constancy of wages*, the working men ought, therefore, under certain circumstances, to combine and struggle for a rise of wages. If he denies this conclusion, he must give up the premise from which it flows. He must not say that the amount of wages is a *constant quantity*, but that, although it cannot and must not *rise*, it can and must *fall*, whenever capital pleases to lower it. If the capitalist pleases to feed you upon potatoes instead of upon meat, and upon oats instead of upon wheat, you must accept his will as a law of political economy, and submit to it. If in one country the rate of wages is higher than in another, in the United States, for example, than in England, you must explain this difference in the rate of wages by a difference between the will of the American capitalist and the will of the English capitalist, a method which would certainly very much simplify, not only the study of economic phenomena, but of all other phenomena.

But even then, we might ask, *why* the will of the American capitalist differs from the will of the English capitalist? And to answer the question you must go beyond the domain of *will*. A person may tell me that God wills one thing in France, and another thing in England. If I summon him to explain this duality of will, he might have the brass to answer me that God wills to have one will in France and another will in England. But our friend Weston is certainly the last man to make an argument of such a complete negation of all reasoning.

The *will* of the capitalist is certainly to take as much as possible. What we have to do is not to talk about his *will*, but to enquire into his *power*, the *limits of that power*, and the *character of those limits*.

2

Production, Wages, Profits

The address Citizen Weston read to us might have been compressed into a nutshell.

All his reasoning amounted to this: If the working class forces the capitalist class to pay five shillings instead of four shillings in the shape of money wages, the capitalist will return in the shape of commodities four shillings' worth instead of five shillings' worth. The working class would have to pay five shillings for what, before the rise of wages, they bought with four shillings. But why is this the case? Why does the capitalist only return four shillings' worth for five shillings? Because the amount of wages is fixed. By why is it fixed at four shillings' worth of commodities? Why not at three, or two, or any other sum? If the limit of the amount of wages is settled by an economical law, independent alike of the will of the capitalist and the will of the working man, the first thing

Citizen Weston had to do was to state that law and prove it. He ought then, moreover, to have proved that the amount of wages actually paid at every given moment always corresponds exactly to the necessary amount of wages, and never deviates from it. If, on the other hand, the given limit of the amount of wages is founded on the *mere will* of the capitalist, or the limits of his avarice, it is an arbitrary limit. There is nothing necessary in it. It may be changed *by* the will of the capitalist, and may, therefore, be changed *against* his will.

Citizen Weston illustrated his theory by telling you that a bowl contains a certain quantity of soup, to be eaten by a certain number of persons, an increase in the broadness of the spoons would produce no increase in the amount of soup. He must allow me to find this illustration rather spoony. It reminded me somewhat of the simile employed by Menenius Agrippa. When the Roman plebeians struck against the Roman patricians, the patrician Agrippa told them that the patrician belly fed the plebeian members of the body politic. Agrippa failed to show that you feed the members of one man by filling the belly of another. Citizen Weston, on his part, has forgotten that the bowl from which the workmen eat is filled with the whole produce of national labour, and that what prevents them fetching more out of it is neither the narrowness of the bowl nor the scantiness of its contents, but only the smallness of their spoons.

By what contrivance is the capitalist enabled to return four shillings' worth for five shillings? By raising the price of the commodity he sells. Now, does a rise and more generally a change in the prices of commodities, do the prices of commodities themselves, depend on the mere will of the capitalist? Or are, on the contrary, certain circumstances wanted to give effect to that will? If not, the ups and downs, the incessant fluctuations of market prices, become an insoluble riddle.

As we suppose that no change whatever has taken place either in the productive powers of labour, or in the amount of capital and labour employed, or in the value of the money wherein the values of products are estimated, but *only a change in the rate of wages*, how could that *rise of wages* affect the *prices of commodities*? Only by affecting the actual proportion between the demand for, and the supply of these commodities.

It is perfectly true that, considered as a whole, the working class spends, and must spend, its income upon *necessaries*. A general rise in the rate of wages would, therefore, produce a rise in the demand for, and consequently in the *market prices of necessaries*. The capitalists who produce these necessaries would be compensated for the risen wages by the rising market prices of their commodities. But how with the other capitalists who do *not* produce necessaries? And you must not fancy them a small body. If you consider that two-thirds of the national produce are consumed by one-fifth of the population—a member of the House of Commons stated it recently to be but one-seventh of the population—you will understand what an immense proportion of the national produce must be produced in the shape of luxuries, or be *exchanged* for luxuries, and what an immense amount of the necessaries themselves must be wasted upon flunkeys, horses, cats, and so forth, a waste we know from experience to become always much limited with the rising prices of necessaries.

Well, what would be the position of those capitalists who do *not* produce necessaries? For the *fall in the rate of profit*, consequent upon the general rise of wages, they could not compensate themselves by a *rise in the price of their commodities*, because the demand for those commodities would not have increased. Their income would have decreased, and from this decreased income they would have to pay more for the same amount of higher-priced necessaries. But this would not be all. As their income had diminished they would have less to spend upon luxuries, and therefore their mutual demand for their respective commodities would diminish. Consequent upon this diminished demand the prices of their commodities would fall. In these branches of industry, therefore, *the rate of profit would fall*, not only in simple proportion to the general rise in the rate of wages, but in the compound ratio of the general rise of wages, the rise in the prices of necessaries, and the fall in the prices of luxuries.

What would be the consequence of *this difference in the rates of profit* for capitals employed in the different branches of industry? Why, the consequence that generally obtains whenever, from whatever reason, the *average rate of profit* comes to differ in different spheres of production. Capital and labour would be transferred from the less remunerative to the more remunerative branches; and this process of transfer would go on until the supply in the one department of industry would have risen proportionately to the increased demand, and would have sunk in the other departments according to the decreased demand. This change effected, the general rate of profit would again be *equalized* in the different branches. As the whole derangement originally arose from a mere change in the proportion of the demand for, and supply of, different commodities, the cause ceasing, the effect would cease, and prices would return to their former level and equilibrium. Instead of being limited to some branches of industry, *the fall in the rate of profit* consequent upon the rise of wages would have become general. According to our supposition, there would have taken place no change in the productive powers of labour, nor in the aggregate amount of production, but *that given amount of production would have changed its form.* A greater part of the produce would exist in the shape of necessaries, a lesser part in the shape of luxuries, or what comes to the same, a lesser part would be exchanged for foreign luxuries, and be consumed in its original form, or, what again comes to the same, a greater part of the native produce would be exchanged for foreign necessaries instead of for luxuries. The general rise in the rate of wages would, therefore, after a temporary disturbance of market prices, only result in a general fall of the rate of profit without any permanent change in the prices of commodities. If I am told that in the previous argument I assume the whole surplus wages to be spent upon necessaries, I answer that I have made the supposition most advantageous to the opinion of Citizen Weston. If the surplus wages were spent upon articles formerly not entering into the consumption of the working men, the real increase of their purchasing power would need no proof. Being, however, only derived from an advance of wages, that increase of their purchasing power must exactly correspond to the decrease of the purchasing power of the capitalists. The *aggregate demand* for commodities would, therefore, not *increase*, but the constituent parts of that demand would *change*. The increasing demand on the one side would be counterbalanced by the decreasing demand on the other side. Thus the aggregate demand remaining stationary, no change whatever could take place in the market prices of commodities. You arrive, therefore, at this dilemma: Either the surplus wages are equally spent upon all articles of consumption—then the expansion of demand on the part of the working class must be compensated by the contraction of demand on the part of the capitalist class—or the surplus wages are only spent upon some articles whose market prices will temporarily rise. The consequent rise in the rate of profit in some, and the consequent fall in the rate of profit in other branches of industry will produce a change in the distribution of capital and labour, going on until the supply is brought up to the increased demand in the one department of industry, and brought down to the diminished demand in the other departments of industry. On the one supposition there will occur no change in the prices of commodities. On the other supposition, after some fluctuations of market prices, the exchangeable values of commodities will subside to the former level. On both suppositions the general rise in the rate of wages will ultimately result in nothing else but a general fall in the rate of profit.

To stir up your powers of imagination Citizen Weston requested you to think of the difficulties which a general rise of English agricultural wages from nine shillings to eighteen shillings would produce. Think, he exclaimed, of the immense rise in the demand for necessaries, and the consequent fearful rise in their prices! Now, all of you know that the average wages of the American agricultural labourer amount to more than double that of the English agricultural labourer, although the prices of agricultural produce are lower in the United States than in the United Kingdom, although the general relations of capital and labour obtain in the United States the same as in England, and although the annual amount of production is much smaller in the United States than in England. Why, then, does our friend ring this alarm bell? Simply to shift the real question before us. A sudden rise of wages from nine shillings to eighteen shillings would be a sudden rise to the amount of 100 percent. Now, we are not at all discussing the question whether the general rate of wages in England could be suddenly increased by 100 percent. We have nothing at all to do with the *magnitude* of the rise, which in every practical instance must depend on, and be suited to, given circumstances. We have only to inquire how a general rise in the rate of wages, even if restricted to one percent, will act.

Dismissing friend Weston's fancy rise of 100 percent, I propose calling your attention to the real rise of wages that took place in Great Britain from 1849 to 1859.

You are all aware of the Ten Hours Bill, or rather Ten-and-a-half Hours Bill, introduced since 1848. This was one of the greatest economical changes we have witnessed. It was a sudden and compulsory rise of wages, not in some local trades, but in the leading industrial branches by which England sways the markets of the world. It was a rise of wages under circumstances singularly unpropitious. Dr. Ure, Professor Senior, and all the other official economical mouthpieces of the middle class,

[The aristocracy was the upper class of Great Britain, while the capitalists composed what was known to Marx as the middle class] *proved*, and I must say upon much stronger grounds than those of our friend Weston, that it would sound the death-knell of English industry. They proved that it not only amounted to a simple rise of wages, but to a rise of wages initiated by, and based upon, a diminution of the quantity of labour employed. They asserted that the twelfth hour you wanted to take from the capitalist was exactly the only hour from which he derived his profit. They threatened a decrease of accumulation, rise of prices, loss of markets, stinting of production, consequent reaction upon wages, ultimate ruin. In fact, they declared Maximillian Robespierre's Maximum Laws[1] to be a small affair compared to it; and they were right in a certain sense. Well, what was the result? A rise in the money wages of the factory operatives, despite the curtailing of the working day, a great increase in the number of factory hands employed, a continuous fall in the prices of their products, a marvellous development in the productive powers of their labour, an unheard-of progressive expansion of the markets for their commodities. In Manchester, at the meeting, in 1860, of the Society for the Advancement of Science, I myself heard

1. The Maximum Law was introduced during the Great French Revolution in 1792, fixing definite price limits for commodities and standard rates of wages. The chief supporters of the Maximum Law were the so-called "madmen" who represented the interests of the urban and village poor. Robespierre, the leader of the Jacobin Party, introduced this law at a time when the Jacobins as a result of tactical considerations had formed a bloc with the "madmen." — *Ed.*

Mr. Newman confess that he, Dr. Ure, Senior, and all other official propounders of economical science had been wrong, while the instinct of the people had been right. I mention Mr. W. Newman, not Professor Francis Newman, because he occupies an eminent position in economical science, as the contributor to, and editor of, Mr. Thomas Tooke's *History of Prices*, that magnificent work which traces the history of prices from 1793 to 1856. If our friend Weston's fixed idea of a fixed amount of wages, a fixed amount of production, a fixed degree of the productive power of labour, a fixed and permanent will of the capitalist, and all his other fixedness and finality were correct, Professor Senior's woeful forebodings would been right, and Robert Owen[2], who already in 1816 proclaimed a general limitation of the working day the first preparatory step to the emancipation of the working class, and actually in the teeth of the general prejudice inaugurated it on his own hook in his cotton factory at New Lanark, would have been wrong.

In the very same period during which the introduction of the Ten Hours Bill, and the rise of wages consequent upon it, occurred, there took place in Great Britain, for reasons which it would be out of place to enumerate here, *a general rise in agricultural wages*. Although it is not required for my immediate purpose, in order not to mislead you, I shall make some preliminary remarks.

---

2. Robert Owen (1771-1858) was a British manufacturer who became a utopian socialist. He introduced in his factory the ten-hour day, and also organised sickness insurance, consumers' co-operative societies, etc. — *Ed.*

If a man got two shillings weekly wages, and if his wages rose to four shillings, the *rate of wages* would have risen by 100 per cent. This would seem a very magnificent thing if expressed as a rise in the *rate of wages*, although the *actual amount of wages*, four shillings weekly, would still remain a wretchedly small, a starvation pittance. You must not, therefore, allow yourselves to be carried away by the high sounding per cents in *rate* of wages. You must always ask: What was the *original* amount?

Moreover, you will understand, that if there were ten men receiving each 2s. per week, five men receiving each 5s., and five men receiving 11s. weekly, the twenty men together would receive 100s., or £5, weekly. If then a rise, say by 20 per cent, upon the *aggregate* sum of their weekly wages took place, there would be an advance from £5 to £6. Taking the average, we might say that the *general rate of wages* had risen by 20 per cent, although, in fact, the wages of the ten men had remained stationary, the wages of the one lot of five men had risen from 5s. To 6s. Only, and the wages of the other lot of five from 55s. To 70s.[3] One half of the men would not have improved at all their position, one quarter would have improved it in an imperceptible degree, and only one quarter would have bettered it really. Still, reckoning by the *average*, the total amount of the wages of those twenty men would have increased by 25 per cent, and as far as the aggregate capital that employs them, and the prices of the commodities they produce,

---

3. These figures, 55s.-70s., refer to the total wages of the group of five men. The wage of each man in the group would increase from 11s. to 14s. — *Ed.*

are concerned, it would be exactly the same as if all of them had equally shared in the average rise of wages. In the case of agricultural labour, the standard wages being very different in the different counties of England and Scotland, the rise affected them very unequally.

Lastly, during the period when that rise of wages took place counteracting influences were at work such as the new taxes consequent upon the Russian war, the extensive demolition of the dwelling-houses of the agricultural labourers, and so forth. Having premised so much, I proceed to state that from 1849 to 1859 there took place a *rise of about 40 percent* in the average rate of the agricultural wages of Great Britain. I could give you ample details in proof of my assertion, but for the present purpose think it sufficient to refer you to the conscientious and critical paper read in 1860 by the late Mr. John C. Morton at the London Society of Arts on "The Forces used in Agriculture." Mr. Morton gives the returns, from bills and other authentic documents, which he had collected from about one hundred farmers, residing in twelve Scotch and thirty-five English counties.

According to our friend Weston's opinion, and taken together with the simultaneous rise in the wages of the factory operatives, there ought to have occurred a tremendous rise in the prices of agricultural produce during the period 1849 to 1859. But what is the fact? Despite the Russian war, and the consecutive unfavourable harvests from 1854 to 1856, the average price of wheat, which is the leading agricultural produce of England, fell from about 3 Pounds per quarter for the years 1838 to 1848 to about 2 Pounds 10 Shillings per quarter for the years 1849 to 1859. This constitutes a fall in the price of wheat of more than 16 percent simultaneously with an average rise of agricultural wages of 40 percent. During the same period, if we compare its end with its beginning, 1859 with 1849, there was a decrease of official pauperism from 934,419 to 860,470, the difference being 73,949; a very small decrease, I grant, and which in the following years was again lost, but still a decrease.

It might be said that, consequent upon the abolition of the Corn Laws, the import of foreign corn was more than doubled during the period from 1849 to 1859, as compared with the period from 1838 to 1848. And what of that? From Citizen Weston's standpoint one would have expected that this sudden, immense, and continuously increasing demand upon foreign markets must have sent up the prices of agricultural produce there to a frightful height, the effect of increased demand remaining the same, whether it comes from without or from within. What was the fact? Apart from some years of failing harvests, during all that period the ruinous fall in the price of corn formed a standing theme of declamation in France; the Americans were again and again compelled to burn their surplus produce; and Russia, if we are to believe Mr. Urquhart, prompted the Civil War in the United States because her agricultural exports were crippled by the Yankee competition in the markets of Europe.

Reduced to its abstract form, Citizen Weston's argument would come to this: Every rise in demand occurs always on the basis of a given amount of production. It can, therefore, *never increase the supply of the articles demanded,* but can *only enhance their money prices.* Now the most common observation shows than an increased demand will, in some instances, leave the market prices of commodities altogether unchanged, and will, in other instances, cause a temporary rise of market prices followed by an increased supply, followed by a reduction of the prices to their original level, and in many cases *below* their original level. Whether the rise of demand springs from surplus wages, or from any other cause, does not at all change the conditions of the problem. From Citizen Weston's standpoint the general phenomenon was as difficult to explain as the phenomenon occurring under the exceptional circumstances of a rise of wages. His argument had, therefore, no peculiar bearing whatever upon the subject we treat. It only expressed his perplexity at accounting for the laws by which an increase of demand produces an increase of supply, instcad of an ultimate rise of market prices.

3

Wages and Currency

On the second day of the debate our friend Weston clothed his old assertions in new forms. He said: Consequent upon a general rise in money wages, more currency will be wanted to pay the same wages. The currency being *fixed*, how can you pay with this fixed currency increased money wages? First the difficulty arose from the fixed amount of commodities accruing to the working man despite his increase of money wages; now it arises from the increased money wages, despite the fixed amount of commodities. Of course, if you reject his original dogma, his secondary grievance will disappear. However, I shall show that this currency question has nothing at all to do with the subject before us.

In your country the mechanism of payments is much more perfected than in any other country of Europe. Thanks to the extent and concentration of the banking system, much less currency is wanted to circulate the same amount of values, and to transact the same or a greater amount of business. For example, as far as wages are concerned, the English factory operative pays his wages weekly to the shopkeeper, who sends them weekly to the banker, who returns them weekly to the manufacturer, who again pays them away to his working men, and so forth. By this contrivance the yearly wages of an operative, say of 52 Pounds, may be paid by one single Sovereign turning round every week in the same circle. Even in England the mechanism is less perfect than in Scotland, and is not everywhere equally perfect; and therefore we find, for example, that in some agricultural districts, much more currency is wanted to circulate a much smaller amount of values.

If you cross the Channel you will find that the *money wages* are much lower than in England, but that they are circulated in Germany, Italy, Switzerland, and France by a *much larger amount of currency*. The same Sovereign will not be so quickly intercepted by the banker or returned to the industrial capitalist; and, therefore, instead of one Sovereign circulating 52 Pounds yearly, you want, perhaps, three Sovereigns to circulate yearly wages to the amount of 25 Pounds. Thus, by comparing continental countries with England, you will see at once that low money wages may require a much larger currency for their circulation than high money wages, and that this is, in fact, a merely technical point, quite foreign to our subject.

According to the best calculations I know, the yearly income of the working class of this country may be estimated at 250,000,000 Pounds. This immense sum is circulated by about three million Pounds. Suppose a rise of wages of fifty per cent to take place. Then, instead of three millions of currency, four and a half million would be wanted. As a very considerable part of the working-man's daily expenses is laid out in silver and copper, that is to say, in mere tokens, whose relative value to gold is arbitrarily fixed by law, like that of inconvertible money paper, a rise of money wages by fifty per cent would, in the extreme case, require and additional circulation of Sovereigns, say to the amount of one million. One million, now dormant, in the shape of bullion or coin, in the cellars of the Bank of England, or of private bankers would circulate. But even the trifling expense resulting from the additional minting or the additional wear and tear of that million might be spared, and would actually be spared, if any friction should arise from the want of the additional currency. All of you know that the currency of this country is divided into two great departments. One sort, supplied by bank-notes of different descriptions, is used in the transactions between dealers and dealers, and the larger payments from consumers to dealers, while another sort of currency, metallic coin, circulates in the retail trade. Although distinct, these two sorts of currency intermix with each other. Thus gold coin, to a very great extent, circulates even in larger payments for all the odd sums under 5 Pounds. If tomorrow 4 Pound notes, or 3 Pound notes, or 2 Pound notes were issued, the gold filling these channels of circulation would at once be driven out of them, and flow into those channels where they would be needed from the increase of money wages. Thus the additional million required by an advance of wages by fifty per cent would be supplied without the addition of one single Sovereign. The same effect might be produced, without one additional bank-note, by an additional bill circulation, as was the case in Lancashire for a very considerable time.

If a general rise in the rate of wages, for example, of 100 per cent, as Citizen Weston supposed it to take place in agricultural wages, would produce a great rise in the prices of necessaries, and, according to his views, require an additional amount of currency not to be procured, *a general fall in wages* must produce the same effect, on the same scale, in the oppo site direction. Well! All of you know that the years 1858 to 1860 were the most prosperous years for the cotton industry, and that peculiarly the year 1860 stands in that respect unrivalled in the annals of commerce, while at the same time all other branches of industry were most flourishing. The wages of the cotton operatives and of all the other working men connected with their trade stood, in 1860, higher than ever before. The American crisis came, and those aggregate wages were suddenly reduced to about one-fourth of their former amount. This would have been in the opposite direction a rise of 400 per cent. If wages rise from five to twenty, we say that they rise by 400 per cent; if they fall from twenty to five, we say that they fall by seventy-five per cent; but the amount of rise in the one and the amount of fall in the other case would be the same, namely, fifteen shillings. This, then, was a sudden change in the rate of wages unprecedented, and at the same time extending over a number of operatives which, if we count all the operatives not only directly engaged in but indirectly dependent upon the cotton trade, was larger by one-half than the number of agricultural labourers. Did the price of wheat fall?

It *rose* from the annual average of 47 shillings 8d per quarter during the three years of 1858-1860 to the annual average of 55 shillings 10d per quarter during the three years 1861-1863. As to the currency, there were coined in the mint in 1861 8,673,323 Pounds, against 3,378,792 Pounds in 1860. That is to say, there were coined 5,294,440 Pounds more in 1861 than in 1860. It is true the bank-note circulation was in 1861 less by 1,319,000 Pounds than in 1860. Take this off. There remains still a surplus of currency for the year 1861, as compared with the prosperity year, 1860, to the amount of 3,975,440 Pounds, or about 4,000,000 Pounds; but the bullion reserve in the Bank of England had simultaneously decreased, not quite to the same, but in an approximating proportion.

Compare the year 1862 with 1842. Apart from the immense increase in the value and amount of commodities circulated, in 1862 the capital paid in regular transactions for shares, loans, etc. for the railways in England and Wales amounted alone to 320,000,000 Pounds, a sum that would have appeared fabulous in 1842. Still, the aggregate amounts in currency in 1862 and 1842 were pretty nearly equal, and generally you will find a tendency to a progressive diminution of currency in the face of enormously increasing value, not only of commodities, but of monetary transactions generally. From our friend Weston's standpoint this is an unsolvable riddle. Looking somewhat deeper into this matter, he would have found that, quite apart from wages, and supposing them to be fixed, the value and mass of the commodities to be circulated, and generally the amount of monetary transactions to be settled, vary daily; that the amount of bank-notes issued varies daily; that the amount of payments realized without the intervention of any money, by the instrumentality of bills, cheques, book-credits, clearing houses, varies daily; that, as far as actual metallic currency is required, the proportion between the coin in circulation and the coin and bullion in reserve or sleeping in the cellars of banks varies daily; that the amount of bullion absorbed by the national circulation and the amount being sent abroad for international circulation vary daily. He would have found that this dogma of a fixed currency is a monstrous error, incompatible with our everyday movement. He would have inquired into the laws which enable a currency to adapt itself to circumstances so continually changing, instead of turning his misconception of the laws of currency into an argument against a rise of wages.

4

Supply and Demand

Our friend Weston accepts the Latin proverb that "*repetitio est mater studio rum,*" that is to say, that repetition is the mother of study, and consequently he repeated his original dogma again under the new form, that the contraction of currency, resulting from an enhancement of wages, would produce a diminution of capital, and so forth. Having already dealt with his currency crotchet, I consider it quite useless to enter upon the imaginary consequences he fancies to flow from his imaginary currency mishap. I shall proceed to at once reduce his *one and the same dogma*, repeated in so many different shapes, to its simplest theoretical form.

The uncritical way in which he has treated his subject will become evident from one single remark. He pleads against a rise of wages or against high wages as the result of such a rise. Now, I ask him: What are high wages and what are low wages?

Why constitute, for example, five shillings weekly low, and twenty shillings weekly high wages? If five is low as compared with twenty, twenty is still lower as compared with two hundred. If a man was to lecture on the thermometer, and commenced by declaiming on high and low degrees, he would impart no knowledge whatever. He must first tell me how the freezing-point is found out, and how the boiling-point, and how these standard points are settled by natural laws, not by the fancy of the sellers or makers of thermometers. Now, in regard to wages and profits, Citizen Weston has not only failed to deduce such standard points from economical laws, but he has not even felt the necessity to look after them. He satisfied himself with the acceptance of the popular slang terms of low and high as something having a fixed meaning, although it is self-evident that wages can only be said to be high or low as compared with a standard by which to measure their magnitudes.

He will be unable to tell me why a certain amount of money is given for a certain amount of labour. If he should answer me, "This was settled by the law of supply and demand," I should ask him, in the first instance, by what law supply and demand are themselves regulated. And such an answer would at once put him out of court. The relations between the supply and demand of labour undergo perpetual change, and with them the market prices of labour. If the demand overshoots the supply wages rise; if the supply overshoots the demand wages sink, although it might in such circumstances be necessary to *test* the real state of demand and supply by a strike, for example, or any other method. But if you accept supply and demand as the law regulating wages, it would be as childish as useless to declaim against a rise of wages, because, according to the supreme law you appeal to, a periodical rise of wages is quite as necessary and legitimate as a periodical fall of wages. If you do *not* accept supply and demand as the law regulating wages, I again repeat the question, why a certain amount of money is given for a certain amount of labour?

But to consider matters more broadly: You would be altogether mistaken in fancying that the value of labour or any other commodity whatever is ultimately fixed by supply and demand. Supply and demand regulate nothing but the temporary *fluctuations* of market prices. They will explain to you why the market price of a commodity rises above or sinks below its *value*, but they can never account for the *value* itself. Suppose supply and demand to equilibrate, or, as the economists call it, to cover each other. Why, the very moment these opposite forces become equal they paralyze each other, and cease to work in the one or other direction. At the moment when supply and demand equilibrate each other, and therefore cease to act, the *market price* of a commodity coincides with its *real value*, with the standard price round which its market prices oscillate. In inquiring into the nature of that VALUE, we have therefore nothing at all to do with the temporary effects on market prices of supply and demand. The same holds true of wages and of the prices of all other commodities.

5

Wages and Prices

Reduced to their simplest theoretical expression, all our friend's arguments resolve themselves into this one dogma: "*The prices of commodities are determined or regulated by wages.*"

I might appeal to practical observation to bear witness against this antiquated and exploded fallacy. I might tell you that the English factory operatives, miners, shipbuilders, and so forth, whose labour is relatively high-priced, undersell by the cheapness of their produce all other nations; while the English agricultural labourer, for example, whose labour is relatively low-priced, is undersold by almost every other nation because of the dearness of his produce. By comparing article with article in the same country, and the commodities of different countries, I might show, apart from some exceptions more apparent than real, that on an average the high-priced labour produces the low-priced, and low priced labour produces the high-priced commodities. This, of course, would not prove that the high price of labour in the one, and its low price in the other instance, are the respective causes of those diametrically opposed effects, but at all events it would prove that the prices of commodities are not ruled by the prices of labour. However, it is quite superfluous for us to employ this empirical method.

It might, perhaps, be denied that Citizen Weston has put forward the dogma: "*The prices of commodities are determined or regulated by wages.*" In point of fact, he has never formulated it. He said, on the contrary, that profit and rent also form constituent parts of the prices of commodities, because it is out of the prices of commodities that not only the working man's wages, but also the capitalist's profits and the landlord's rents must be paid. But how in his idea are prices formed? First by wages. Then an additional percentage is joined to the price on behalf of the capitalist, and another additional percentage on behalf of the landlord. Suppose the wages of the labour employed in the production of a commodity to be ten. If the rate of profit was 100 per cent, to the wages advanced the capitalist would add ten, and if the rate of rent was also 100 per cent upon the wages, there would be added ten more, and the aggregate price of the commodity would amount to thirty. But such a determination of prices would be simply their determination by wages. If wages in the above case rose to twenty, the price of the commodity would rise to sixty, and so forth. Consequently all the superannuated writers on political economy who propounded the dogma that wages regulate prices, have tried to prove it by treating profit and rent *as mere additional percentages upon wages*. None of them were, of course, able to reduce the limits of those percentages to any economic law. They seem, on the contrary, to think profits settled by tradition, custom, the will of the capitalist, or by some other equally arbitrary and inexplicable method. If they assert that they are settled by the competition between the capitalists, they say nothing. That competition is sure to equalize the different rates of profit in different trades, or reduce them to one average level, but it can never determine the level itself, or the general rate of profit.

What do we mean by saying that the prices of the commodities are determined by wages? Wages being but a name for the price of labour, we mean that the prices of commodities are regulated by the price of labour. As "price" is exchangeable value—and in speaking of value I speak always of exchangeable value—is exchangeable *value expressed in money*, the proposition comes to this, that "the *value of commodities* is determined by the value of labour," or that "the *value of labour is the general measure of value*."

But how, then, is the "*value of labour*" itself determined? Here we come to a standstill. Of course, we come to a standstill if we try reasoning logically, yet the propounders of that doctrine make short work of logical scruples. Take our friend Weston, for example. First he told us that wages regulate the price of commodities and that consequently when wages rise prices must rise. Then he turned round to show us that a rise of wages will be no good because the prices of commodities had risen, and because wages were indeed measured by the prices of the commodities upon which they are spent. Thus we begin by saying that the value of labour determines the value of commodities, and we wind up by saying that the value of commodities determines the value of labour. Thus we move to and fro in the most vicious circle, and arrive at no conclusion at all.

On the whole, it is evident that by making the value of one commodity, say labour, corn, or any other commodity, the general measure and regulator of value, we only shift the difficulty, since we determine one value by another, which on its side wants to be determined.

The dogma that "wages determine the price of commodities," expressed in its most abstract terms, comes to this, that "value is determined by value," and this tautology means that, in fact, we know nothing at all about value. Accepting this premise, all reasoning about the general laws of political economy turns into mere twaddle. It was, therefore, the great merit of Ricardo that in his work on *the principles of political economy*, published in 1817, he fundamentally destroyed the old popular, and worn-out fallacy that "wages determine prices," a fallacy which Adam Smith and his French predecessors had spurned in the really scientific parts of their researches, but which they reproduced in their more exoterical and vulgarizing chapters.

6

Value and Labour

Citizens, I have now arrived at a point where I must enter upon the real development of the question. I cannot promise to do this in a very satisfactory way, because to do so I should be obliged to go over the whole field of political economy. I can, as the French would say, but "effleurer la question," touch upon the main points. The first question we have to put is: What is the *value* of a commodity? How is it determined?

At first sight it would seem that the value of a commodity is a thing quite *relative*, and not to be settled without considering one commodity in its relations to all other commodities. In fact, in speaking of the value, the value in exchange of a commodity, we mean the proportional quantities in which it exchanges with all other commodities. But then a rises the question: How are the proportions in which commodities exchange with each other regulated? We know from experience that these proportions vary infinitely. Taking one single commodity, wheat, for instance, we shall find that a quarter of wheat exchanges in almost countless variations of proportion with different commodities. Yet, *its value remaining always the same*, whether expressed in silk, gold, or any other commodity, it must be something distinct from, and independent of, these *different rates of exchange* with different articles. It must be possible to express, in a very different form, these various equations with various commodities.

Besides, if I say a quarter of wheat exchanges with iron in a certain proportion, or the value of a quarter of wheat is expressed in a certain amount of iron, I say that the value of wheat and its equivalent in iron are equal to *some third thing*, which is neither wheat nor iron, because I suppose them to express the same magnitude in two different shapes. Either of them, the wheat or the iron, must, therefore, independently of the other, be reducible to this third thing which is their common measure.

To elucidate this point I shall recur to a very simple geometrical illustration. In comparing the areas of triangles of all possible forms and magnitudes, or comparing triangles with rectangles, or any other rectilinear figure, how do we proceed? We reduce the area of any triangle whatever to an expression quite different from its visible form. Having found from the nature of the triangle that its area is equal to half the product of its base by its height, we can then compare the different values of all sorts of triangles, and of all rectilinear figures whatever, because all of them may be resolved into a certain number of triangles.

The same mode of procedure must obtain with the values of commodities. We must be able to reduce all of them to an expression common to all, and distinguishing them only by the proportions in which they contain that identical measure.

As the *exchangeable values* of commodities are only *social functions* of those things, and have nothing at all to do with the *natural* qualities, we must first ask: What is the common *social substance* of all commodities? It is *labour*. To produce a commodity a certain amount of labour must be bestowed upon it, or worked up in it. And I say not only *labour*, but *social labour*. A man who produces an article for his own immediate use, to consume it himself, creates a *product*, but not a *commodity*. As a self-sustaining producer he has nothing to do with society. But to produce a *commodity*, a man must not only produce an article satisfying some *social* want, but his labour itself must form part and parcel of the total sum of labour expended by society. It must be subordinate to the *division of labour within society*. It is nothing without the other divisions of labour, and on its part is required to *integrate* them.

If we consider *commodities as values*, we consider them exclusively under the single aspect of *realized, fixed*, or, if you like, *crystallized social labour*. In this respect they can *differ* only by representing greater or smaller quantities of labour, as, for example, a greater amount of labour may be worked up in a silken handkerchief than in a brick. But how does one measure *quantities of labour*? By the *time the labour lasts*, in measuring the labour by the hour, the day, etc. Of course, to apply this measure, all sorts of labour are reduced to average or simple labour as their unit. We arrive, therefore, at this conclusion. A commodity has *a value*, because it is a *crystallization of social labour*. The *greatness* of its value, or its *relative* value, depends upon the greater or less amount of that social substance contained in it; that is to say, on the relative mass of labour necessary for its production. The *relative values of commodities* are, therefore, determined by the *respective quantities or amounts of labour, worked up, realized, fixed in them*. The *correlative* quantities of commodities which can be produced in the *same time of labour* are *equal*. Or the value of one commodity is to the value of another commodity as the quantity of labour fixed in the one is to the quantity of labour fixed in the other.

I suspect that many of you will ask: Does then, indeed, there exist such a vast or any difference whatever, between determining the values of commodities by *wages*, and determining them by the *relative quantities of labour* necessary for their production? You must, however, be aware that the *reward* for labour, and *quantity* of labour, are quite disparate things. Suppose, for example, *equal quantities of labour* to be fixed in one quarter of wheat and one ounce of gold. I resort to the example because it was used by Benjamin Franklin in his first Essay published in 1721, and entitled *A Modest Enquiry into the Nature and Necessity of a Paper Currency*, where he, one of the first, hit upon the true nature of value.

Well. We suppose, then, that one quarter of wheat and one ounce of gold are *equal values* or *equivalents*, because they are *crystallizations of equal amounts of average labour*, of so many days' or so many weeks' labour respectively fixed in them.

In thus determining the relative values of gold and corn, do we refer in any way whatever to the *wages* of the agricultural labourer and the miner? Not a bit. We leave it quite *indeterminate* how their day's or their week's labour was paid, or even whether wage labour was employed at all. If it was, wages may have been very unequal. The labourer whose labour is realized in the quarter of wheat may receive two bushels only, and the labourer employed in mining may receive one-half of the ounce of gold. Or, supposing their wages to be equal, they may deviate in all possible proportions from the values of the commodities produced by them. They may amount to one-fourth, one-fifth, or any other proportional part of the one quarter of corn or the one ounce of gold. Their *wages* can, of course, not *exceed*, not be *more* than the values of the commodities they produced, but they can be *less* in every possible degree. Their *wages* will be *limited* by the *values* of the products, but the *values of their products* will not be limited by the wages. And above all, the values, the relative values of corn and gold, for example, will have been settled without any regard whatever to the value of the labour employed, that is to say, to *wages*. To determine the values of commodities by the *relative quantities of labour fixed in them*, is, therefore, a thing quite different from the tautological method of determining the values of commodities by the value of labour, or by *wages*. This point, however, will be further elucidated in the progress of our inquiry.

In calculating the exchangeable value of a commodity we must add to the quantity of labour *previously* worked up in the raw material of the commodity, and the labour bestowed on the implements, tools, machinery, and buildings, with which such labour is assisted. For example, the value of a certain amount of cotton yarn is the crystallization of the quantity of labour added to the cotton during the spinning process, the quantity of labour previously realized in the cotton itself, the quantity of labour realized in the coal, oil, and other auxiliary substances used, the quantity of labour fixed in the steam-engine, the spindles, the factory building, and so forth. Instruments of production properly so-called, such as tools, machinery, buildings, serve again and again for longer or shorter period during repeated processes of production. If they were used up at once, like the raw material, their whole value would at once be transferred to the commodities they assist in producing. But as a spindle, for example, is but gradually used up, an average calculation is made, based upon the average time it lasts, and its average waste or wear and tear during a certain period, say a day. In this way we calculate how much of the value of the spindle is transferred to the yarn daily spin, and how much, therefore, of the total amount of labour realized in a pound of yarn, for example, is due to the quantity of labour previously realized in the spindle. For our present purpose it is not necessary to dwell any longer upon this point.

It might seem that if the value of a commodity is determined by the *quantity of labour bestowed upon its production*, the lazier a man, or the clumsier a man, the more valuable his commodity, because the greater the time of labour required for finishing the commodity. This, however, would be a sad mistake. You will recollect that I used the word "*social* labour," and many points are involved in this qualification of "*social*."

In saying that the value of a commodity is determined by the *quantity of labour* worked up or crystallized in it, we mean *the quantity of labour necessary* for its production in a given state of society, under certain social average conditions of production, with a given social average intensity, and average skill of the labour employed. When, in England, the power-loom came to compete with the hand-loom, only half the former time of labour was wanted to convert a given amount of yarn into a yard of cotton or cloth. The poor hand-loom weaver now worked seventeen or eighteen hours daily, instead of the nine or ten hours he had worked before. Still the product of twenty hours of his labour represented now only ten social hours of labour, or ten hours of labour socially necessary for the conversion of a certain amount of yarn into textile stuffs. His product of twenty hours had, therefore, no more value than his former product of ten hours.

If then the quantity of socially necessary labour realized in commodities regulates their exchangeable values, every increase in the quantity of labour wanted for the production of a commodity must augment its value, as every diminution must lower it.

If the respective quantities of labour necessary for the production of the respective commodities remained constant, their relative values also would be constant. But such is not the case. The quantity of labour necessary for the production of a commodity changes continuously with the changes in the productive powers of labour, the more produce is finished in a given time of labour; and the smaller the productive powers of labour, the less produce is finished in the same time. If, for example, in the progress of population it should become necessary to cultivate less fertile soils, the same amount of produce would be only attainable by a greater amount of labour spent, and the value of agricultural produce would consequently rise. On the other hand, if, with the modern means of production, a single spinner converts into yarn, during one working day, many thousand times the amount of cotton which he could have spun during the same time with the spinning wheel, it is evident that every single pound of cotton will absorb many thousand times less of spinning labour than it did before, and consequently, the value added by spinning to every single pound of cotton will be a thousand times less than before. The value of yarn will sink accordingly.

Apart from the different natural energies and acquired working abilities of different peoples, the productive powers of labour must principally depend:—

Firstly. Upon the *natural* conditions of labour, such as fertility of soil, mines, and so forth.

Secondly. Upon the progressive improvement of the *social powers of labour*, such as are derived from production on a grand scale, concentration of capital and combination of labour, subdivision of labour, machinery, improved methods, appliance of chemical and other natural agencies, shortening of time and space by means of communication and transport, and every other contrivance by which science presses natural agencies into the service of labour, and by which the social or co-operative character of labour is developed. The greater the productive powers of labour, the less labour is bestowed upon a given amount of produce; hence the smaller the value of the produce. The smaller the productive powers of labour, the more labour is bestowed upon the same amount of produce; hence the greater its value. As a general law we may, therefore, set it down that:—

The values of commodities are directly as the times of labour employed in their production, and are inversely as the productive powers of the labour employed.

Having till now only spoken of *value*, I shall add a few words about *price*, which is a peculiar form assumed by value.

Price, taken by itself, is nothing but the *monetary expression of value*. The values of all commodities of the country, for example, are expressed in gold prices, while on the Continent they are mainly expressed in silver prices. The value of gold or silver, like that of all other commodities is regulated by the quantity of labour necessary for getting them. You exchange a certain amount of your national products, in which a certain amount of your national labour is crystallized, for the produce of the gold and silver producing countries, in which a certain quantity of *their* labour is crystallized. It is in this way, in fact by barter, that you learn to express in gold and silver the values of all commodities, that is the respective quantities of labour bestowed upon them. Looking somewhat closer into the *monetary expression of value*, or what comes to the same, the conversion of value into price, you will find that it is a process by which you give to the *values* of all commodities an *independent* and *homogeneous form*, or by which you express them as quantities of equal social labour. So far as it is but the monetary expression of value, price has been called *natural price* by Adam Smith, "*prix necessaire*" by the French physiocrats.

What then is the relation between *value* and *market prices*, or between *natural prices* and *market prices*? You all know that the *market price* is the *same* for all commodities of the same kind, however the conditions of production may differ for the individual producers. The market price expresses only the *average amount of social labour* necessary, under the average conditions of production, to supply the market with a certain mass of a certain article. It is calculated upon the whole lot of a commodity of a certain description.

So far the *market price* of a commodity coincides with its *value*. On the other hand, the oscillations of market prices, rising now over, sinking now under the value or natural price, depend upon the fluctuations of supply and demand. The deviations of market prices from values are continual, but as Adam Smith says:

> "The natural price is the central price to which the prices of commodities are continually gravitating. Different accidents may sometimes keep them suspended a good deal above it, and sometimes force them down even somewhat below it. But whatever may be the obstacles which hinder them from settling in this centre of repose and continuance, they are constantly tending towards it."

I cannot now sift this matter. It suffices to say the *if* supply and demand equilibrate each other, the market prices of commodities will correspond with their natural prices, that is to say with their values, as determined by the respective quantities of labour required for their production. But supply and demand *must* constantly tend to equilibrate each other, although they do so only by compensating one fluctuation by another, a rise by a fall, and *vice versa*. If instead of considering only the daily fluctuations you analyze the movement of market prices for longer periods, as Mr. Tooke, for example, has done in his *History of Prices*, you will find that the fluctuations of market prices, their deviations from values, their ups and downs, paralyze and compensate each other; so that apart from the effect of monopolies and some other modifications I must now pass by, all descriptions of commodities are, on average, sold at their respective *values* or natural prices. The average periods during which the fluctuations of market prices compensate each other are different for different kinds of commodities, because with one kind it is easier to adapt supply to demand than with the other.

If then, speaking broadly, and embracing somewhat longer periods, all descriptions of commodities sell at their respective values, it is nonsense to suppose that profit, not in individual cases; but that the constant and usual profits of different trades spring from the prices of commodities, or selling them at a price over and above their *value*. The absurdity of this notion becomes evident if it is generalized. What a man would constantly win as a seller he would constantly lose as a purchaser. It would not do to say that there are men who are buyers without being sellers, or consumers without being producers. What these people pay to the producers, they must first get from them for nothing. If a man first takes your money and afterwards returns that money in buying your commodities, you will never enrich yourselves by selling your commodities too dear to that same man. This sort of transaction might diminish a loss, but would never help in realizing a profit. To explain, therefore, the *general nature of profits*, you must start from the theorem that, on an average, commodities are *sold at their real values*, and that *profits are derived from selling them at their values*, that is, in proportion to the quantity of labour realized in them. If you cannot explain profit upon this supposition, you cannot explain it at all. This seems paradox and contrary to every-day observation. It is also paradox that the earth moves round the sun, and that water consists of two highly inflammable gases. Scientific truth is always paradox, if judged by every-day experience, which catches only the delusive appearance of things.

7

Labour Power

Having now, as far as it could be done in such a cursory manner, analyzed the nature of *value*, of the *value of any commodity whatever*, we must turn our attention to the specific *value of labour*. And here, again, I must startle you by a seeming paradox. All of you feel sure that what they daily sell is their Labour; that, therefore, Labour has a price, and that, the price of a commodity being only the monetary expression of its value, there must certainly exist such a thing as the *value of labour*. However, there exists no such thing as the *value of labour* in the common acceptance of the word. We have seen that the amount of necessary labour crystallized in a commodity constitutes its value. Now, applying this notion of value, how could we define, say, the value of a ten hours working day? How much labour is contained in that day? Ten hours' labour.

To say that the value of a ten hours working day is equal to ten hours' labour, or the quantity of labour contained in it, would be a tautological and, moreover, a nonsensical expression. Of course, having once found out the true but hidden sense of the expression "*value of labour*," we shall be able to interpret this irrational, and seemingly impossible application of value, in the same way that, having once made sure of the real movement of the celestial bodies, we shall be able to explain their apparent or merely phenomenal movements.

What the working man sells is not directly his *labour*, but his *labouring power*, the temporary disposal of which he makes over to the capitalist. This is so much the case that I do not know whether by the English Laws, but certainly by some Continental Laws, the *maximum time* is fixed for which a man is allowed to sell his labouring power. If allowed to do so for any indefinite period whatever, slavery would be immediately restored. Such a sale, if it comprised his lifetime, for example, would make him at once the lifelong slave of his employer.

One of the oldest economists and most original philosophers of England—Thomas Hobbes—has already, in his Leviathan, instinctively hit upon this point overlooked by all his successors. He says: "*the value or worth of a man* is, as in all other things, his *price*: that is so much as would be given for the *use of his power*." Proceeding from this basis, we shall be able to determine the *value of labour* as that of all other commodities.

But before doing so, we might ask, how does this strange phenomenon arise, that we find on the market a set of buyers, possessed of land, machinery, raw material, and the means of subsistence, all of them, save land in its crude state, the *products of labour*, and on the other hand, a set of sellers who have nothing to sell except their labouring power, their working arms and brains? That the one set buys continually in order to make a profit and enrich themselves, while the other set continually sells in order to earn their livelihood? The inquiry into this question would be an inquiry into what the economists call "*previous or original accumulation*," but which ought to be called *original expropriation*. We should find that this so-called *original accumulation* means nothing but a series of historical processes, resulting in a *decomposition* of the *original union* existing between the labouring Man and his Instruments of Labour. Such an inquiry, however, lies beyond the pale of my present subject. The *separation* between the Man of Labour and the Instruments of Labour once established, such a state of things will maintain itself and reproduce itself upon a constantly increasing scale, until a new and fundamental revolution in the mode of production should again overturn it, and restore the original union in a new historical form.

What, then, is the *value of labouring power*?

Like that of every other commodity, its value is determined by the quantity of labour necessary to produce it. The labouring power of a man exists only in his living individuality. A certain mass of necessaries must be consumed by a man to grow up and maintain his life. But the man, like the machine, will wear out, and must be replaced by another man. Beside the mass of necessaries required for *his own* maintenance, he wants another amount of necessaries to bring up a certain quota of children that are to replace him on the labour market and to perpetuate the race of labourers. Moreover, to develop his labouring power, and acquire a given skill, another amount of values must be spent. For our purpose it suffices to consider only *average* labour, the costs of whose education and development are vanishing magnitudes. Still I must seize upon this occasion to state that, as the costs of producing labouring powers of different quality differ, so much differ the values of the labouring powers employed in different trades. The cry for an *equality of wages* rests, therefore, upon a mistake, is an inane wish never to be fulfilled. It is an offspring of that false and superficial radicalism that accepts premises and tries to evade conclusions. Upon the basis of the wages system the value of labouring power is settled like that of every other commodity; and as different kinds of labouring power have different values, or require different quantities of labour for their production, they *must* fetch different prices in the labour market. To clamour for *equal or even equitable retribution* on the basis of the wages system is the same as to clamour for *freedom* on the basis of the slavery system. What you think just or equitable is out of the question. The question is: What is necessary and unavoidable with a given system of production? After what has been said, it will be seen that the *value of labouring power* is determined by the *value of the necessaries* required to produce, develop, maintain, and perpetuate the labouring power.

8

Production of Surplus Value

Now suppose that the average amount of the daily necessaries of a labouring man require *six hours of average labour* for their production. Suppose, moreover, six hours of average labour to be also realized in a quantity of gold equal to 3s. Then 3s. Would be the *price*, or the monetary expression of the *daily value* of that man's *labouring power*. If he worked daily six hours he would daily produce a value sufficient to buy the average amount of his daily necessaries, or to maintain himself as a labouring man.

But our man is a wages labourer. He must, therefore, sell his labouring power to a capitalist. If he sells it at 3s. Daily, or 18s. Weekly, he sells it at its value. Suppose him to be a spinner. If he works six hours daily he will add to the cotton a value of 3s. Daily. This value, daily added by him, would be an exact equivalent for the wages, or the price of his labouring power, received daily. But in that case *no surplus value* or *surplus produce* whatever would go to the capitalist. Here, then, we come to the rub.

In buying the labouring power of the workman, and paying its value, the capitalist, like every other purchaser, has acquired the right to consume or use the commodity bought. You consume or use the labouring power of a man by making him work, as you consume or use a machine by making it run. By buying the daily or weekly value of the labouring power of the workman, the capitalist has, therefore, acquired the right to use or make that labouring power during the *whole day or week.* The working day or the working week has, of course, certain limits, but those we shall afterwards look more closely at.

For the present I want to turn your attention to one decisive point. The *value* of the labouring power is determined by the quantity of labour necessary to maintain or reproduce it, but the *use* of that labouring power is only limited by the active energies and physical strength of the labourer. The daily or weekly *value* of the labouring power is quite distinct from the daily or weekly exercise of that power, the same as the food a horse wants and the time it can carry the horseman are quite distinct. The quantity of labour by which the *value* of the workman's labouring power is limited forms by no means a limit to the quantity of labour which his labouring power is apt to perform. Take the example of our spinner. We have seen that, to daily reproduce his labouring power, he must daily reproduce a value of three shillings, which he will do by working six hours daily. But this does not disable him from working ten or twelve or more hours a day. But by paying the daily or weekly *value* of the spinner's labouring power the capitalist has acquired the right of using that labouring power during *the whole day or week*. He will, therefore, make him work say, daily, *twelve hours. Over and above* the six hours required to replace his wages, or the value of his labouring power, he will, therefore, have to work *six other hours*, which I shall call hours of *surplus labour*, which surplus labour will realize itself in a *surplus value* and a *surplus produce*. If our spinner, for example, by his daily labour of six hours, added three shillings' value to the cotton, a value forming an exact equivalent to his wages, he will, in twelve hours, add six shillings' worth to the cotton, and produce *a proportional surplus of yarn*. As he has sold his labouring power to the capitalist, the whole value of produce created by him belongs to the capitalist, the owner *pro tem*. Of his labouring power. By advancing three shillings, the capitalist will, therefore, realize a value of six shillings, because, advancing a value in which six hours of labour are crystallized, he will receive in return a value in which twelve hours of labour are crystallized. By repeating this same process daily, the capitalist will daily advance three shillings and daily pocket six shillings, one half of which will go to pay wages anew, and the other half of which will form *surplus value*, for which the capitalist pays no equivalent. It is this *sort of exchange between capital and labour* upon which capitalistic production, or the wages system, is founded, and which must constantly result in reproducing the working man as a working man, and the capitalist as a capitalist.

The rate of surplus value, all other circumstances remaining the same, will depend on the proportion between that part of the working day necessary to reproduce the value of the labouring power and the *surplus time* or *surplus labour* performed for the capitalist. It will, therefore, depend on the *ratio in which the working day is prolonged over and above that extent*, by working which the working man would only reproduce the value of his labouring power, or replace his wages.

9

Value of Labour

We must now return to the expression, "*value, or price of labour.*" We have seen that, in fact, it is only the value of the labouring power, measured by the values of commodities necessary for its maintenance. But since the workman receives his wages *after* his labour is performed, and knows, moreover, that what he actually gives to the capitalist is his labour, the value or price of his labouring power necessarily appears to him as the *price* or *value of his labour itself.* If the price of his labouring power is three shillings, in which six hours of labour are realized, and if he works twelve hours, he necessarily considers these three shillings as the value or price of twelve hours of labour, although these twelve hours of labour realize themselves in a value of six shillings. A double consequence flows from this.

Firstly. The *value or price of the labouring power* takes the semblance of the *price or value of labour itself*, although, strictly speaking, value and price of labour are senseless terms.

Secondly. Although one part only of the workman's daily labour is *paid*, while the other part is *unpaid*, and while that unpaid or surplus labour constitutes exactly the fund out of which *surplus value* or *profit* is formed, it seems as if the aggregate labour was paid labour.

This false appearance distinguishes *wages labour* from other *historical* forms of labour. On the basis of the wages system even the *unpaid* labour seems to be *paid* labour. With the *slave*, on the contrary, even that part of his labour which is paid appears to be unpaid. Of course, in order to work the slave must live, and one part of his working day goes to replace the value of his own maintenance. But since no bargain is struck between him and his master, and no acts of selling and buying are going on between the two parties, all his labour seems to be given away for nothing.

Take, on the other hand, the peasant serf, such as he, I might say, until yesterday existed in the whole of East of Europe. This peasant worked, for example, three days for himself on his own field or the field allotted to him, and the three subsequent days he performed compulsory and gratuitous labour on the estate of his lord. Here, then, the paid and unpaid parts of labour were sensibly separated, separated in time and space; and our Liberals overflowed with moral indignation at the preposterous notion of making a man work for nothing.

In point of fact, however, whether a man works three days of the week for himself on his own field and three days for nothing on the estate of his lord, or whether he works in the factory or the workshop six hours daily for himself and six for his employer, comes to the same, although in the latter case the paid and unpaid portions of labour are inseparably mixed up with each other, and the nature of the whole transaction is completely masked by the *intervention of a contract* and the *pay* received at the end of the week. The gratuitous labour appears to be voluntarily given in the one instance, and to be compulsory in the other. That makes all the difference.

In using the word "*value of labour,*" I shall only use it as a popular slang term for "*value of labouring power.*"

10

Profit is Made by Selling a Commodity at its Value

Suppose an average hour of labour to be realized in a value equal to sixpence, or twelve average hours of labour to be realized in six shillings. Suppose, further, the value of labour to be three shillings or the produce of six hours' labour. If, then, in the raw material, machinery, and so forth, used up in a commodity, twenty-four hours of average labour were realized, its value would amount to twelve shillings. If, moreover, the workman employed by the capitalist added twelve hours of labour to those means of production, these twelve hours would be realized in an additional value of six shillings. The *total value of the product* would, therefore, amount to thirty-six hours of realized labour, and be equal to eighteen shillings. But as the value of labour, or the wages paid to the workman, would be three shillings only, no equivalent would have been paid by the capitalist for the six hours of surplus labour worked by the workman, and realized in the value of the commodity. By selling this commodity at its value for eighteen shillings, the capitalist would, therefore, realize a value of three shillings, for which had paid no equivalent. These three shillings would constitute the surplus value or profit pocketed by him. The capitalist would consequently realize the profit of three shillings, not by selling his commodity at a price *over and above* its value, but by selling it *at its real value.*

The value of a commodity is determined by the *total quantity of labour* contained in it. But part of that quantity of labour is realized in a value for which and equivalent has been paid in the form of wages; part of it is realized in a value for which NO equivalent has been paid. Part of the labour contained in the commodity is *paid* labour; part is *unpaid* labour. By selling, therefore, the commodity *at its value*, that is, as the crystallization of the *total quantity of labour* bestowed upon it, the capitalist must necessarily sell it at a profit. He sells not only what has cost him an equivalent, but he sells also what has cost him nothing, although it has cost his workman labour. The cost of the commodity to the capitalist and its real cost are different things.

I repeat, therefore, that normal and average profits are made by selling commodities not *above*, but *at their real values.*

11

The Different Parts into which Surplus Value is Decomposed

The *surplus value*, or that part of the total value of the commodity in which the *surplus labour* or *unpaid labour* of the working man is realized, I call *profit*. The whole of that profit is not pocketed by the employing capitalist. The monopoly of land enables the landlord to take one part of that *surplus value*, under the name of *rent*, whether the land is used for agricultural buildings or railways, or for any other productive purpose. On the other hand, the very fact that the possession of the *instruments of labour* enables the employing capitalist to produce a *surplus value*, or, what comes to the same, to *appropriate to himself a certain amount of unpaid labour*, enables the owner of the means of labour, which he lends wholly or partly to the employing capitalist—enables, in one word, the money-lending capitalist to claim for himself under the name of *interest* another part of that surplus value, so that there remains to the employing capitalist *as such* only what is called *industrial* or *commercial profit.*

By what laws this division of the total amount of surplus value amongst the three categories of people is regulated is a question quite foreign to our subject. This much, however, results from what has been stated.

Rent, interest, and industrial profit are only different names for different parts of the *surplus value* of the commodity, or the *unpaid labour enclosed in it*, and they are *equally derived from this source and from this source alone.* They are not derived from *land* as such or from *capital* as such, but land and capital enable their owners to get their respective shares out of the surplus value extracted by the employing capitalist from the labourer. For the labourer himself it is a matter of subordinate importance whether that surplus value, the result of his surplus labour, or unpaid labour, is altogether pocketed by the employing capitalist, or whether the latter is obliged to pay portions of it, under the name of rent and interest, away to third parties. Suppose the employing capitalist to use only his own capital and to be his own landlord, then the whole surplus value would go into his pocket.

It is the employing capitalist who immediately extracts from the labourer this surplus value, whatever part of it he may ultimately be able to keep for himself. Upon this relation, therefore between the employing capitalist and the wages labourer the whole wages system and the whole present system of production hinge. Some of the citizens who took part in our debate were, there, wrong in trying to mince matters, and to treat this fundamental relation between the employing capitalist and the working man as a secondary question, although they were right in stating that, under given circumstances, a rise of prices might affect in very unequal degrees the employing capitalist, the landlord, the moneyed capitalist, and, if you please, the tax-gatherer.

Another consequence follows from what has been stated.

That part of the value of the commodity which represents only the value of the raw materials, the machinery, in one word, the value of the means of production used up, forms *no revenue* at all, but replaces *only capital.* But, apart from this, it is false that the other part of the value of the commodity *which forms revenue*, or may be spent in the form of wages, profits, rent, interest, is *constituted* by the value of wages, the value of rent, the value of profits, and so forth. We shall, in the first instance, discard wages, and only treat industrial profits, interest, and rent. We have just seen that the *surplus value* contained in the *commodity*, or that part of its value in which *unpaid labour* is realized, resolves itself into different fractions, bearing three different names.

But it would be quite the reverse of the truth to say that its value is *composed* of, or *formed* by, the *addition* of the *independent values of these three constituents.*

If one hour of labour realizes itself in a value of sixpence, if the working day of the labourer comprises twelve hours, if half of this time is unpaid labour, that surplus labour will add to the commodity a *surplus value* of three shillings, that is of value for which no equivalent has been paid. This surplus value of three shillings constitutes the *whole fund* which the employing capitalist may divide, in whatever proportions, with the landlord and the money-lender. The value of these three shillings constitutes the limit of the value they have to divide amongst them. But it is not the employing capitalist who adds to the value of the commodity an arbitrary value for his profit, to which another value is added for the landlord, and so forth, so that the addition of these arbitrarily fixed values would constitute the total value. You see, therefore, the fallacy of the popular notion, which confounds the *decomposition of a given value* into three parts, with the *formation* of that value by the addition of three *independent* values, thus converting the aggregate value, from which rent, profit, and interest are derived, into an arbitrary magnitude.

If the total profit realized by a capitalist is equal to 100 Pounds, we call this sum, considered as *absolute* magnitude, the *amount of profit.* But if we calculate the ratio which those 100 Pounds bear to the capital advanced, we call this *relative* magnitude, the *rate of profit.* It is evident that this rate of profit may be expressed in a double way.

Suppose 100 Pounds to be the capital *advanced in wages.* If the surplus value created is also 100 Pounds—and this would show us that half the working day of the labourer consists of *unpaid* labour—and if we measured this profit by the value of the capital advanced in wages, we should say that the *rate of profit* amounted to one hundred percent, because the value advanced would be one hundred and the value realized would be two hundred.

If, on the other hand, we should not only consider the *capital advanced in wages*, but the *total capital* advanced, say, for example, 500 Pounds, of which 400 Pounds represented the value of raw materials, machinery, and so forth, we should say that the *rate of profit* amounted only to twenty percent, because the profit of one hundred would be but the fifth part of the *total* capital advanced.

The first mode of expressing the rate of profit is the only one which shows you the real ratio between paid and unpaid labour, the real degree of the *exploitation* (you must allow me this French word) *of labour*. The other mode of expression is that in common use, and is, indeed, appropriate for certain purposes. At all events, it is very useful for concealing the degree in which the capitalist extracts gratuitous labour from the workman.

In the remarks I have still to make I shall use the word *profit* for the whole amount of the surplus value extracted by the capitalist without any regard to the division of that surplus value between different parties, and in using the words *rate of profit*, I shall always measure profits by the value of the capital advanced in wages.

12

General Relation of Profits, Wages, and Prices

Deduct from the value of a commodity the value replacing the value of the raw materials and other means of production used upon it, that is to say, deduct the value representing the *past* labour contained in it, and the remainder of its value will resolve into the quantity of labour added by the working man *last* employed. If that working man works twelve hours daily, if twelve hours of average labour crystallize themselves in an amount of gold equal to six shillings, this additional value of six shillings is the *only* value his labour will have created. This given value, determined by the time of his labour, is the only fund from which both he and the capitalist have to draw their respective shares or dividends, the only value to be divided into wages and profits. It is evident that this value itself will not be altered by the variable proportions in which it may be divided amongst the two parties. There will also be nothing changed if in the place of one working man you put the whole working population, twelve million working days, for example, instead of one.

Since the capitalist and workman have only to divide this limited value, that is, the value measured by the total labour of the working man, the more the one gets the less will the other get, and *vice versa*. Whenever a quantity is given, one part of it will increase inversely as the other decreases. If the wages change, profits will change in an opposite direction. If wages fall, profits will rise; and if wages rise, profits will fall. If the working man, on our former supposition, gets three shillings, equal to one half of the value he has created, or if his whole working day consists half of paid, half of unpaid labour, the *rate of profit* will be 100 percent, because the capitalist would also get three shillings. If the working man receives only two shillings, or works only one third of the whole day for himself, the capitalist will get four shillings, and the rate of profit will be 200 per cent. If the working man receives four shillings, the capitalist will only receive two, and the rate of profit would sink to 50 percent, but all these variations will not affect the value of the commodity. A general rise of wages would, therefore, result in a fall of the general rate of profit, but not affect values.

But although the values of commodities, which must ultimately regulate their market prices, are exclusively determined by the total quantities of labour fixed in them, and not by the division of that quantity into paid and unpaid labour, it by no means follows that the values of the single commodities, or lots of commodities, produced during twelve hours, for example, will remain constant. The *number* or mass of commodities produced in a given time of labour, or by a given quantity of labour, depends upon the *productive power* of the labour employed, and not upon its *extent* or length. With one degree of the productive power of spinning labour, for example, a working day of twelve hours may produce twelve pounds of yarn, with a lesser degree of productive power only two pounds. If then twelve hours' average labour were realized in the value of six shillings in the one case, the twelve pounds of yarn would cost six shillings, in the other case the two pounds of yarn would also cost six shillings. One pound of yarn would, therefore, cost sixpence in the one case, and three shillings in the other. The difference of price would result from the difference in the productive powers of labour employed. One hour of labour would be realized in one pound of yarn with the greater productive power, while with the smaller productive power, six hours of labour would be realized in one pound of yarn. The price of a pound of yarn would, in the one instance, be only sixpence, although wages were relatively high and the rate of profit low; it would be three shillings in the other instance, although wages were low and the rate of profit high. This would be so because the price of the pound of yarn is regulated by the *total amount of labour worked up in it*, and not by the *proportional division of that total amount into paid and unpaid labour*. The fact I have mentioned before that high-price labour may produce cheap, and low-priced labour may produce dear commodities, loses, therefore, its paradoxical appearance. It is only the expression of the general law that the value of a commodity is regulated by the quantity of labour worked up in it, and the quantity of labour worked up in it depends altogether upon the productive powers of labour employed, and will therefore, vary with every variation in the productivity of labour.

13

Main Cases of Attempts at Raising Wages or Resisting their Fall

Let us now seriously consider the main cases in which a rise of wages is attempted or a reduction of wages resisted.

1. We have seen that the *value of the labouring power*, or in more popular parlance, the *value of labour*, is determined by the value of necessaries, or the quantity of labour required to produce them.

If, then, in a given country the value of the daily average necessaries of the labourer represented six hours of labour expressed in three shillings, the labourer would have to work six hours daily to produce an equivalent for this daily maintenance. If the whole working day was twelve hours, the capitalist would pay him the value of his labour by paying him three shillings. Half the working day would be unpaid labour, and the rate of profit would amount to 100 percent. But now suppose that, consequent upon a decrease of productivity, more labour should be wanted to produce, say, the same amount of agricultural produce, so that the price of the average daily necessaries should rise from three to four shillings. In that case the *value* of labour would rise by one third, or 33 1/3 percent. Eight hours of the working day would be required to produce an equivalent for the daily maintenance of the labourer, according to his old standard of living. The surplus labour would therefore sink from six hours to four, and the rate of profit from 100 to 50 percent. But in insisting upon a rise of wages, the labourer would only insist upon getting the *increased value of his labour*, like every other seller of a commodity, who, the costs of his commodities having increased, tries to get its increased value paid. If wages did not rise, or not sufficiently rise, to compensate for the increased values of necessaries, the *price* of labour would sink below the *value of labour*, and the labourer's standard of life would deteriorate.

But a change might also take place in an opposite direction. By virtue of the increased productivity of labour, the same amount of the average daily necessaries might sink from three to two shillings, or only four hours out of the working day, instead of six, be wanted to reproduce an equivalent for the value of the daily necessaries. The working man would now be able to buy with two shillings as many necessaries as he did before with three shillings. Indeed, the *value of labour* would have sunk, but diminished value would command the same amount of commodities as before. Then profits would rise from three to four shillings, and the rate of profit from 100 to 200 percent. Although the labourer's absolute standard of life would have remained the same, his *relative* wages, and there with his relative social position, as compared with that of the capitalist, would have been lowered. If the working man should resist that reduction of relative wages, he would only try to get some share in the increased productive powers of his own labour, and to maintain his former relative position in the social scale. Thus, after the abolition of the Corn Laws, and in flagrant violation of the most solemn pledges given during the anti-corn law agitation, the English factory lords generally reduced wages ten per cent. The resistance of the workmen was at first baffled, but, consequent upon circumstances I cannot now enter upon, the ten per cent lost were afterwards regained.

2. The *values* of necessaries, and consequently the *value of labour*, might remain the same, but a change might occur in their *money prices*, consequent upon a previous change in the *value of money*. By the discovery of more fertile mines and so forth, two ounces of gold might, for example, cost no more labour to produce than one ounce did before. The *value* of gold would then be depreciated by one half, or fifty per cent. As the *values* of all other commodities would then be expressed in twice their former *money prices*, so also the same with the *value of labour*. Twelve hours of labour, formerly expressed in six shillings, would now be expressed in twelve shillings. If the working man's wages should remain three shillings, instead of rising to six shillings, the *money price of his labour* would only

be equal to *half the value of his labour*, and his standard of life would fearfully deteriorate. This would also happen in a greater or lesser degree if his wages should rise, but not proportionately to the fall in the value of gold. In such a case nothing would have been changed, either in the productive powers of labour, or in supply and demand, or in values.

Nothing would have changed except the money *names* of those values. To say that in such a case the workman ought not to insist upon a proportionate rise of wages, is to say that he must be content to be paid with names, instead of with things. All past history proves that whenever such a depreciation of money occurs, the capitalists are on the alert to seize this opportunity for defrauding the workman. A very large school of political economists assert that, consequent upon the new discoveries of gold lands, the better working of silver mines, and the cheaper supply of quicksilver, the value of precious metals has again depreciated. This would explain the general and simultaneous attempts on the Continent at a rise of wages.

3. We have till now supposed that the *working day* has given limits. The working day, however, has, by itself, no constant limits. It is the constant tendency of capital to stretch it to its utmost physically possible length, because in the same degree surplus labour, and consequently the profit resulting there from, will be increased. The more capital succeeds in prolonging the working day, the greater the amount of other peoples' labour it will appropriate.

During the seventeenth and even the first two thirds of the eighteenth century a ten hours' working day was the normal working day all over England. During the anti-Jacobin war, which was in fact a war waged by the British barons against the British working masses, capital celebrated its bacchanalia, and prolonged the working day from ten to twelve, fourteen, eighteen hours. Malthus, by no means a man whom you would suspect of a maudlin sentimentalism declared in a pamphlet, published about 1815, that if this sort of thing was to go on the life of the nation would be attacked at its very source. A few years before the general introduction of newly-invented machinery, about 1765, a pamphlet appeared in England under the title, *An Essay On Trade*. The anonymous author, an avowed enemy of the working classes, declaims on the necessity of expanding the limits of the working day. Amongst other means to this end, he proposes *working houses*, which, he says, ought to be "Houses of Terror." And what is the length of the working he prescribes for these "Houses of Terror"? *Twelve hours*, the very same time which in 1832 was declared by capitalists, political economists, and ministers to be not only the existing but the necessary time of labour for a child under twelve years.

By selling his labouring power, and he must do so under the present system, the working man makes over to the capitalist the consumption of that power, but within certain rational limits. He sells his labouring power in order to maintain it, apart from its natural wear and tear, but not to destroy it. In selling his labouring power at its daily or weekly value, it is understood that in one day or one week that labouring power shall not be submitted to two days' or two weeks' waste or wear and tear. Take a machine worth 1000 Pounds. If it is used up in ten years it will add to the value of the commodities in whose production it assists 100 Pounds yearly. If it is used up in five years it will add 200 Pounds yearly, or the value of its annual wear and tear is in inverse ratio to the quickness with which it is consumed. But this distinguishes the working man from the machine. Machinery does not wear out exactly in the same ratio in which it is used. Man, on the contrary, decays in a greater ratio than would be visible from the mere numerical addition of work.

In their attempts at reducing the working day to its former rational dimensions, or, where they cannot enforce a legal fixation of a normal working day, at checking overwork by a rise of wages, a rise not only in proportion to the surplus time exacted, but in a greater proportion, working men fulfil only a duty to themselves and their race. They only set limits to the tyrannical usurpations of capital. Time is the room of human development. A man who has no free time to dispose of, whose whole lifetime, apart from the mere physical interruptions by sleep, meals, and so forth, is absorbed by his labour for the capitalist, is less than a beast of burden. He is a mere machine for producing Foreign Wealth, broken in body and brutalized in mind. Yet the whole history of modern industry shows that capital, if not checked, will recklessly and ruthlessly work to cast down the whole working class to this utmost state of degradation.

In prolonging the working day the capitalist may pay *higher wages* and still lower the *value of labour*, if the rise of wages does not correspond to the greater amount of labour extracted, and the quicker decay of the labouring power thus caused. This may be done in another way. Your middle-class statisticians will tell you, for instance, that the average wages of factory families in Lancashire has risen. They forget that instead of the labour of the man, the head of the family, his wife and perhaps three or four children are now thrown under the Juggernaut wheels of capital, and that the rise of the aggregate wages does not correspond to the aggregate surplus labour extracted from the family.

Even with given limits of the working day, such as they now exist in all branches of industry subjected to the factory laws, a rise of wages may become necessary, if only to keep up the old standard *value of labour*. By increasing the *intensity* of labour, a man may be made to expend as much vital force in one hour as he formerly did in two. This has, to a certain degree, been effected in the trades, placed under the Factory Acts, by the acceleration of machinery, and the greater number of working machines which a single individual has now to superintend. If the increase in the intensity of labour or the mass of labour spent in an hour keeps some fair proportion to the decrease in the extent of the working day, the working man will still be the winner. If this limit is overshot, he loses in one form what he has gained in another, and ten hours of labour may then become as ruinous as twelve hours were before. In checking this tendency of capital, by struggling for a rise of wages corresponding to the rising intensity of labour, the working man only resists the depreciation of his labour and the deterioration of his race.

4. All of you know that, from reasons I have not now to explain, capitalistic production moves through certain periodical

cycles. It moves through a state of quiescence, growing animation, prosperity, overtrade, crisis, and stagnation. The market prices of commodities, and the market rates of profit, follow these phases, now sinking below their averages, now rising above them.

Considering the whole cycle, you will find that one deviation of the market price is being compensated by the other, and that, taking the average of the cycle, the market prices of commodities are regulated by their values. Well! During the phases of sinking market prices and the phases of crisis and stagnation, the working man, if not thrown out of employment altogether, is sure to have his wages lowered. Not to be defrauded, he must, even with such a fall of market prices, debate with the capitalist in what proportional degree a fall of wages has become necessary. If, during the phases of prosperity, when extra profits are made, he did not battle for a rise of wages, he would, taking the average of one industrial cycle, not even receive his *average wages*, or the *value* of his labour. It is the utmost height of folly to demand, that while his wages are necessarily affected by the adverse phases of the cycle, he should exclude himself from compensation during the prosperous phases of the cycle. Generally, the *values* of all commodities are only realized by the compensation of the continuously changing market prices, springing from the continuous fluctuations of demand and supply. On the basis of the present system labour is only a commodity like others. It must, therefore, pass through the same fluctuations to fetch an average price corresponding to its value.

It would be absurd to treat it on the one hand as a commodity, and to want on the other hand to exempt it from the laws which regulate the prices of commodities. The slave receives a permanent and fixed amount of maintenance; the wage-labourer does not. He must try to get a rise of wages in the one instance, if only to compensate for a fall of wages in the other. If he resigned himself to accept the will, the dictates of the capitalist as a permanent economical law, he would share in all the miseries of the slave, without the security of the slave.

5. In all the cases I have considered, and they form ninety-nine out of a hundred, you have seen that a struggle for a rise of wages follows only in the track of *previous* changes, and is the necessary offspring of previous changes in the amount of production, the productive powers of labour, the value of labour, the value of money, the extent or the intensity of labour extracted, the fluctuations of market prices, dependent upon the fluctuations of demand and supply, and consistent with the different phases of the industrial cycle; in one word, as reactions of labour against the previous action of capital. By treating the struggle for a rise of wages independently of all these circumstances, by looking only upon the change of wages, and overlooking all other changes from which they emanate, you proceed from a false premise in order to arrive at false conclusions.

14

The Struggle Between Capital and Labour and its Results

1. Having shown that the periodical resistance on the part of the working men against a reduction of wages, and their periodical attempts at getting a rise of wages, are inseparable from the wages system, and dictated by the very fact of labour being assimilated to commodities, and therefore subject to the laws, regulating the general movement of prices; having furthermore, shown that a general rise of wages would result in a fall in the general rate of profit, but not affect the average prices of commodities, or their values, the question now ultimately arises, how far, in this incessant struggle between capital and labour, the latter is likely to prove successful.

I might answer by a generalization, and say that, as with all other commodities, so with labour, its *market price* will, in the long run, adapt itself to its *value*; that, therefore, despite all the ups and downs, and do what he may, the working man will, on an average, only receive the value of his labour, which resolves into the value of his labouring power, which is determined by the value of the necessaries required for its maintenance and reproduction, which value of necessaries finally is regulated by the quantity of labour wanted to produce them.

But there are some peculiar features which distinguish the *value of the labouring power, or the value of labour*, from the values of all other commodities. The value of the labouring power is formed by two elements – the one merely physical, the other historical or social. Its *ultimate limit* is determined by the *physical* element, that is to say, to maintain and reproduce itself, to perpetuate its physical existence, the working class must receive the necessaries absolutely indispensable for living and multiplying. The *value* of those indispensable necessaries forms, therefore, the ultimate limit of the *value of labour*. On the other hand, the length of the working day is also limited by ultimate, although very elastic boundaries. Its ultimate limit is given by the physical force of the labouring man. If the daily exhaustion of his vital forces exceeds a certain degree, it cannot be exerted anew, day by day.

However, as I said, this limit is very elastic. A quick succession of unhealthy and short-lived generations will keep the labour market as well supplied as a series of vigorous and long-lived generations. Besides this mere physical element, the value of labour is in every country determined by a *traditional standard of life*. It is not mere physical life, but it is the satisfaction of certain wants springing from the social conditions in which people are placed and reared up. The English standard of life may be reduced to the Irish standard; the standard of life of a German peasant to that of a Livonian peasant. The important part which historical tradition and social habitude play in this respect, you may learn from Mr. Thornton's work on *over-population*, where he shows that the average wages in different agricultural districts of England still nowadays differ more or less according to the more or less favourable circumstances under which the districts have emerged from the state of serfdom.

This historical or social element, entering into the value of labour, may be expanded, or contracted, or altogether extinguished, so that nothing remains but the *physical limit.* During the time of the anti-Jacobin war, undertaken, as the incorrigible tax-eater and sinecurist, old George Rose, used to say, to save the comforts of our holy religion from the inroads of the French infidels, the honest English farmers, so tenderly handled in a former chapter of ours, depressed the wages of the agricultural labourers even beneath that *mere physical minimum*, but made up by Poor Laws the remainder necessary for the physical perpetuation of the race. This was a glorious way to convert the wages labourer into a slave, and Shakespeare's proud yeoman into a pauper.

By comparing the standard wages or values of labour in different countries, and by comparing them in different historical epochs of the same country, you will find that the *value of labour* itself is not a fixed but a variable magnitude, even supposing the values of all other commodities to remain constant.

A similar comparison would prove that not only the *market rates* of profit change, but its *average* rates.

But as to *profits*, there exists no law which determines their *minimum*. We cannot say what is the ultimate limit of their decrease. And why cannot we fix that limit? Because, although we can fix the *minimum* of wages, we cannot fix their *maximum*.

We can only say that, the limits of the working day being given, the *maximum of profit* corresponds to the *physical minimum of wages*; and that wages being given, the *maximum of profit* corresponds to such a prolongation of the working day as is compatible with the physical forces of the labourer. The maximum of profit is therefore limited by the physical minimum of wages and the physical maximum of the working day. It is evident that between the two limits of the *maximum rate of profit* an immense scale of variations is possible. The fixation of its actual degree is only settled by the continuous struggle between capital and labour, the capitalist constantly tending to reduce wages to their physical minimum, and to extend the working day to its physical maximum, while the working man constantly presses in the opposite direction.

The matter resolves itself into a question of the respective powers of the combatants.

2. As to the *limitation of the working day* in England, as in all other countries, it has never been settled except by *legislative interference*. Without the working men's continuous pressure from without that interference would never have taken place. But at all events, the result was not to be attained by private settlement between the working men and the capitalists.

This very necessity of *general political action* affords the proof that in its merely economical action capital is the stronger side.

As to the *limits* of the *value of labour*, its actual settlement always depends upon supply and demand, I mean the demand for labour on the part of capital, and the supply of labour by the working men. In colonial countries the law of supply and demand favours the working man. Hence the relatively high standard of wages in the United States. Capital may there try its utmost. It cannot prevent the labour market from being continuously emptied by the continuous conversion of wages labourers into independent, self-sustaining peasants. The position of a wages labourer is for a very large part of the American people but a probational state, which they are sure to leave within a longer or shorter term. To mend this colonial state of things the paternal British Government accepted for some time what is called the modern colonization theory, which consists in putting an artificial high price upon colonial land, in order to prevent the too quick conversion of the wages labourer into the independent peasant.

But let us now come to old civilized countries, in which capital domineers over the whole process of production. Take, for example, the rise in England of agricultural wages from 1849 to 1859. What was its consequence? The farmers could not, as our friend Weston would have advised them, raise the value of wheat, nor even its market prices. They had, on the contrary, to submit to their fall. But during these eleven years they introduced machinery of all sorts, adopted more scientific methods, converted part of arable land into pasture, increased the size of farms, and with this the scale of production, and by these and other processes diminishing the demand for labour by increasing its productive power, made the agricultural population again relatively redundant. This is the general method in which a reaction, quicker or slower, of capital against a rise of wages takes place in old, settled countries. Ricardo has justly remarked that machinery is in constant competition with labour, and can often be only introduced when the price of labour has reached a certain height, but the appliance of machinery is but one of the many methods for increasing the productive powers of labour. The very same development which makes common labour relatively redundant simplifies, on the other hand, skilled labour, and thus depreciates it.

The same law obtains in another form. With the development of the productive powers of labour the accumulation of capital will be accelerated, even despite a relatively high rate of wages. Hence, one might infer, as Adam Smith, in whose days modern industry was still in its infancy, did infer, that the accelerated accumulation of capital must turn the balance in favour of the working man, by securing a growing demand for his labour. From this same standpoint many contemporary writers have wondered that English capital having grown in that last twenty years so much quicker than English population, wages should not have been more enhanced. But simultaneously with the progress of accumulation there takes place a *progressive change in the composition of capital.* That part of the aggregate capital which consists of fixed capital, machinery, raw materials, means of production in all possible forms, progressively increases as compared with the other part of capital, which is laid out in wages or in the purchase of labour. This law has been stated in a more or less accurate manner by Mr. Barton, Ricardo, Sismondi, Professor Richard Jones, Professor Ramsey, Cherbuilliez, and others.

If the proportion of these two elements of capital was originally one to one, it will, in the progress of industry, become five to one, and so forth. If of a total capital of 600, 300 is laid out in instruments, raw materials, and so forth, and 300 in wages, the total capital wants only to be doubled to create a demand for 600 working men instead of for 300. But if of a capital of 600, 500 is laid out in machinery, materials, and so forth and 100 only in wages, the same capital must increase from 600 to 3,600 in order to create a demand for 600 workmen instead of 300. In the progress of industry the demand for labour keeps, therefore, no pace with the accumulation of capital. It will still increase, but increase in a constantly diminishing ratio as compared with the increase of capital.

These few hints will suffice to show that the very development of modern industry must progressively turn the scale in favour of the capitalist against the working man, and that consequently the general tendency of capitalistic production is not to raise, but to sink the average standard of wages, or to push the *value of labour* more or less to its *minimum limit.* Such being the tendency of *things* in this system, is this saying that the working class ought to renounce their resistance against the encroachments of capital, and abandon their attempts at making the best of the occasional chances for their temporary improvement? If they did, they would be degraded to one level mass of broken wretches past salvation. I think I have shown that their struggles for the standard of wages are incidents inseparable from the whole wages system, that in 99 cases out of 100 their efforts at raising wages are only efforts at maintaining the given value of labour, and that the necessity of debating their price with the capitalist is inherent to their condition of having to sell themselves as commodities. By cowardly giving way in their everyday conflict with capital, they would certainly disqualify themselves for the initiating of any larger movement.

At the same time, and quite apart from the general servitude involved in the wages system, the working class ought not to exaggerate to themselves the ultimate working of these everyday struggles. They ought not to forget that they are fighting with effects, but not with the causes of those effects; that they are retarding the downward movement, but not changing its direction; that they are applying palliatives, not curing the malady. They ought, therefore, not to be exclusively absorbed in these unavoidable guerilla fights incessantly springing up from the never ceasing encroachments of capital or changes of the market. They ought to understand that, with all the miseries it imposes upon them, the present system simultaneously engenders the *material conditions* and the *social forms* necessary for an economical reconstruction of society. Instead of the *conservative* motto: *"A fair day's wage for a fair day's work!"* they ought to inscribe on their banner the *revolutionary* watchword: *"Abolition of the wages system!"*

After this very long and, I fear, tedious exposition, which I was obliged to enter into to do some justice to the subject matter, I shall conclude by proposing the following resolutions:

Firstly. A general rise in the rate of wages would result in a fall of the general rate of profit, but, broadly speaking, not affect the prices of commodities.

Secondly. The general tendency of capitalist production is not to raise, but to sink the average standard of wages.

Thirdly. Trades Unions work well as centres of resistance against the encroachments of capital. They fail partially from an injudicious use of their power. They fail generally from limiting themselves to a guerilla war against the effects of the existing system, instead of simultaneously trying to change it, instead of using their organized forces as a lever for the final emancipation of the working class that is to say the ultimate abolition of the wages system.

OTHER BOOKS YOU MAY LIKE

OTHER BOOKS YOU MAY LIKE

OTHER BOOKS YOU MAY LIKE

- The Magic of Faith by Joseph Murphy, ISBN: 9789388118743
- The Miracles of Your Mind by Joseph Murphy, ISBN: 9788180320743
- The Mysterious Affair at Styles by Agatha Christie, ISBN: 9789390492510
- The Origin of Species by Charles Darwin, ISBN: 9788180320453
- The Plague by Albert Camus, ISBN: 9788194764892
- The Power of Awareness by Neville Goddard, ISBN: 9789387669406
- The Power of Positive Thinking by Norman Vincent Peale, ISBN: 9789388118569
- The Problem of Increasing Human Energy by Nikola Tesla, ISBN: 9789354990953
- The Prophet by Kahlil Gibran, ISBN: 9789380914022
- The Psychopathology of Everyday Life by Sigmund Freud, ISBN: 9789388118071
- The Pursuit of God by AW Tozer, ISBN: 9789389157147
- The Railway Children by E Nesbit, ISBN: 9789354990960
- The Red Badge of Courage by Stephen Crane, ISBN: 9789354990977
- The Sound and the Fury by William Faulkner, ISBN: 9789390492572
- The Stranger by Albert Camus, ISBN: 9789390492589
- The Sun Also Rises by Ernest Hemingway, ISBN: 9789354990984
- The Yoga Sutras of Patanjali by Patanjali, ISBN: 9789389716351
- Their Eyes Were Watching God by Zora Neale Hurston, ISBN: 9788194764885
- Think and Grow Rich by Napoleon Hill, ISBN: 9788180320255
- Thought Vibration by William Walker Atkinson, ISBN: 9789389157154
- To the Lighthouse by Virginia Woolf, ISBN: 9789390492190
- Who were the Shudras by Dr B.R. Ambedkar, ISBN: 9789354991028
- World's Best Short Stories: Volume 1 by Various Authors, ISBN: 9789390492275
- Wuthering Heights by Emily Brontë, ISBN: 9788193545898
- Your Faith is Your Fortune by Neville Goddard, ISBN: 9789389157161
- Zen in the Art of Archery by Eugen Herrigel, ISBN: 9789354991059